HORSES IN ART

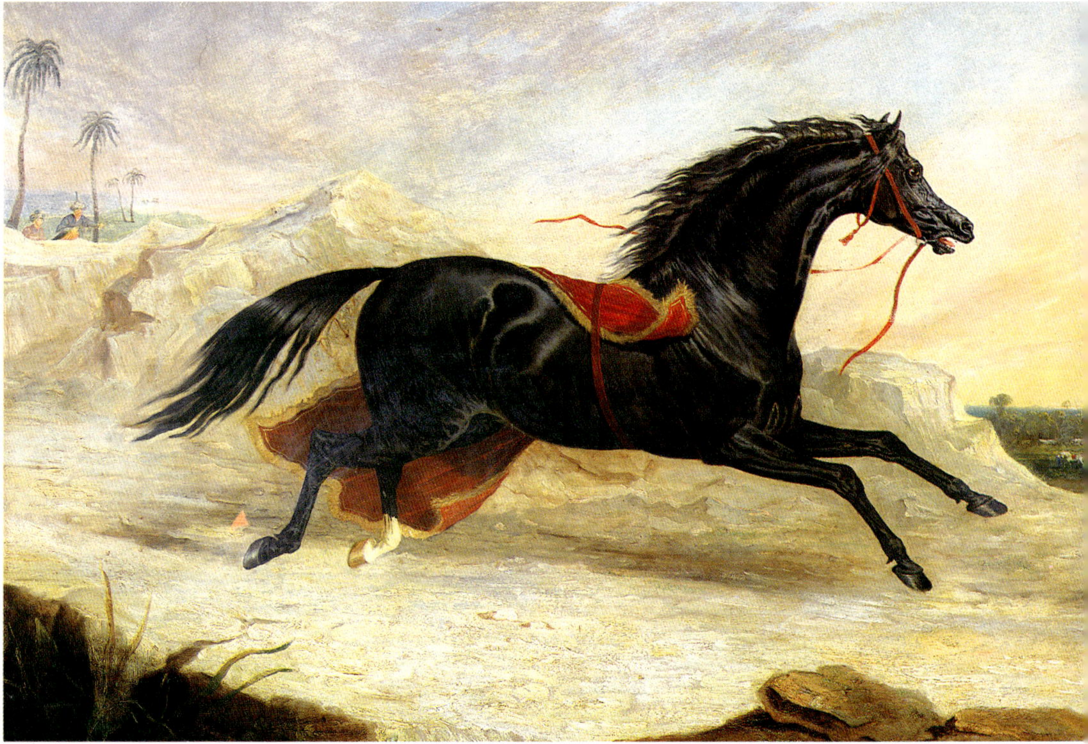

John Herring Snr.(1795 – 1865), *Arabs Chasing a Loose Horse* (detail).

HORSES IN ART

Introduced & compiled by
CHRISTINE O'BRIEN

Picture selection by Julia Brown

STUDIO EDITIONS
LONDON

This edition published 1994 by
Studio Editions Ltd
Princess House, 50 Eastcastle Street
London, W1N 7AP, England

Printed and bound in Singapore

ISBN 1 85891 176 1

INTRODUCTION

Of all the animals domesticated by man, the horse has served the widest variety of purposes. It has provided transport, both as a mount and as a draught animal; it has acted as a formidable engine of war; it has been a sporting companion on hunting field and racecourse. Among many cultures, horses have also been the subject of myths and legends, in which they have symbolized wisdom, courage, strength and mystery. Throughout history, men and women have portrayed all these aspects of the horse in their art, sometimes with affection, sometimes with detachment, but always with a sense of awe at their beauty.

It remains uncertain who the earliest horsemen were, but archaeological evidence suggests that they probably lived in India or China. According to Brahmin mythology, the first human to be created was given a horse to ride; and Chinese ceramics dating back over 5000 years show horses both

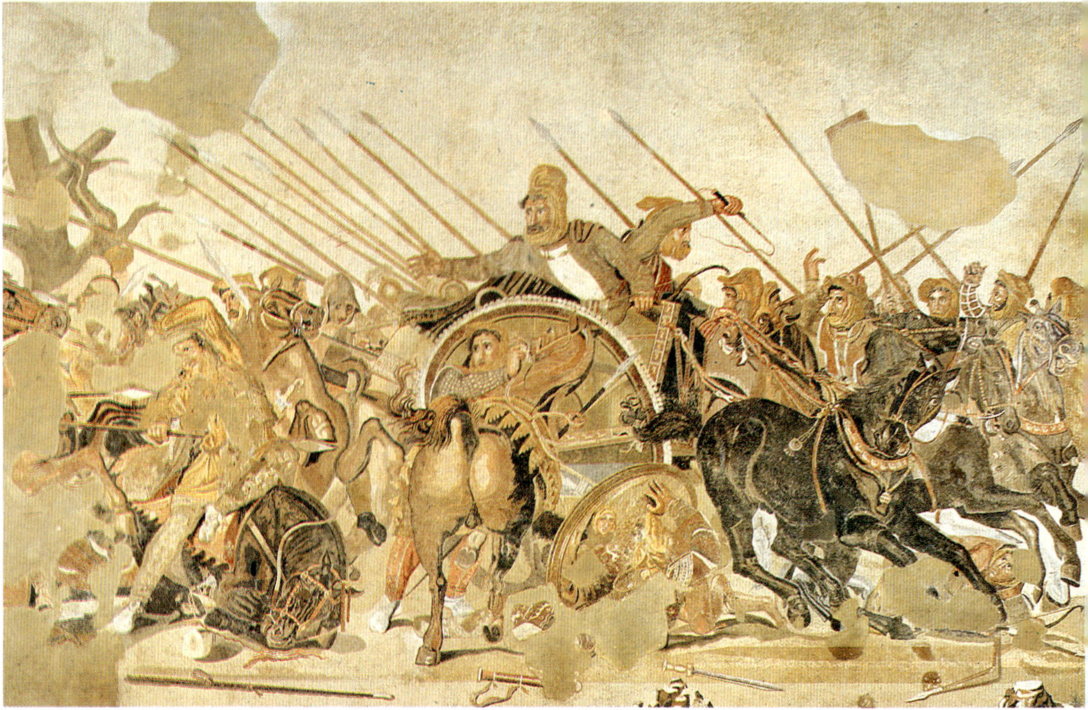

Roman mosaic, *The Battle of Alexander* (detail). Four powerful horses draw a chariot into battle, trampling the foe under foot.

with riders and in harness. The ancient Mediterranean empires of Egypt, Persia, Greece and Rome all deployed cavalry and war-chariots to great effect in their military campaigns, and their use was recorded in sculpture, wall painting and mosaics. Later, the rapid spread of Islam both eastwards into Central Asia and westwards into North Africa and Europe was due in large part to the skill of those mounted warriors whose stylized horses feature in Persian miniature painting (*see* Plate 7).

For the European painters of the Middle Ages the horse was a creature of nobility and power, which could be identified with its owner by heraldic trappings. The mighty chargers which rode into battle or the tournament were expected to carry up to 500lb (250kg) of protective armour as well as their riders. In the hands of the Italian painter Paolo Uccello (*see* Plate 2), these vast animals became geometrical figures, their muscular structure reduced to solid blocks of colour. Even for less martial pursuits, such as hunting, noblemen appear to have valued horses of considerable size. Andrea Mantegna's fresco in the Camera degli Sposi (Bride's Chamber) in the Duke of Mantua's palace shows a heroic animal of statuesque beauty (*see* Plate 3). Indeed, the Duke of Mantua was so proud of his stable of stallions that he had a whole room covered with their portraits.

During the Renaissance, artists were concerned to paint and sketch from life, but the association between horses and heroism continued. Subsequently many formal portraits of kings and queens, aristocrats and generals showed them mounted on a horse, as if to underline their elevated position in society and mastery over the forces of nature.

In the eighteenth century, the wealthy owners of famous hunters and racehorses commissioned both sporting scenes and more idealized, almost classical portraits to show off their prize thoroughbreds. George Stubbs, one of the acknowledged masters of animal painting at this time, had a detailed knowledge of equine anatomy and published a book on the subject full of meticulous drawings. In his paintings, however, the accuracy of his observation was never dry or academic, even when he was depicting a scene of static formality. His awareness of the elegance and energy of horses is evident in every kind of composition, from the idyllic calm of *Mares and Foals without a Background* (*see* Plate 9) to the ferocity of a struggle between a horse and lion.

The spread of portable firearms during the sixteenth and seventeenth centuries meant that by Stubbs' day the medieval charger had been replaced in battle by a much faster, more nimble kind of mount. The

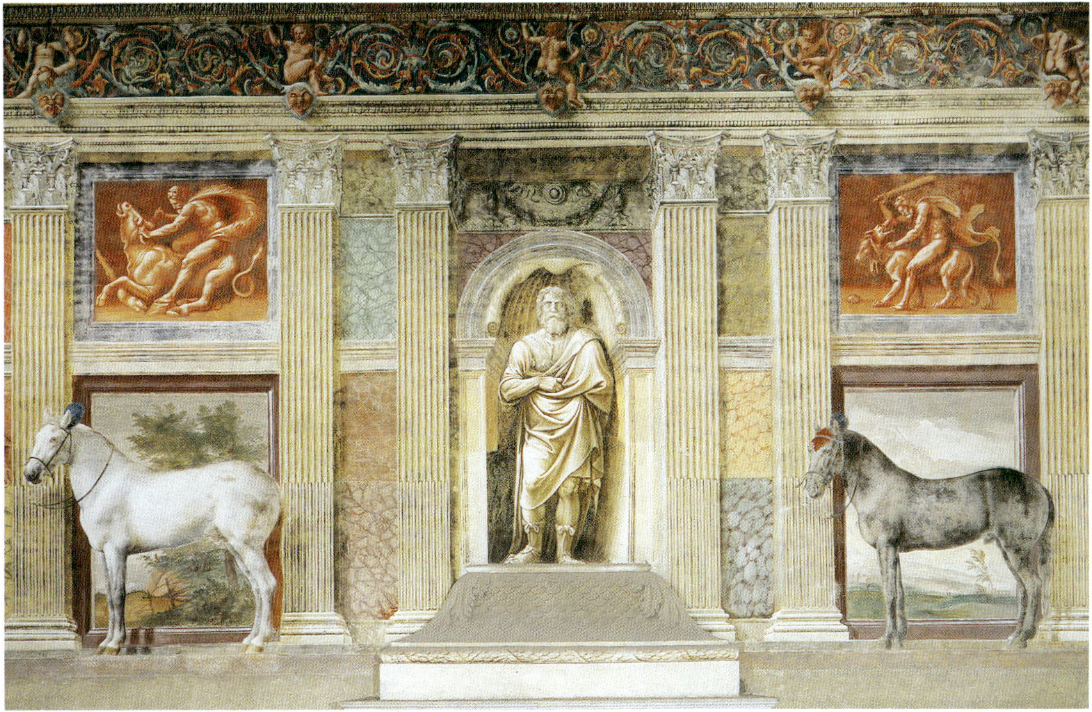

Rinaldo Montovano and Benedetto Pagni, fresco detail, 1527–28, from the Sala dei Cavalli, Palazzo del Té, Mantua. Representations of the Labours of Hercules appear above the horses.

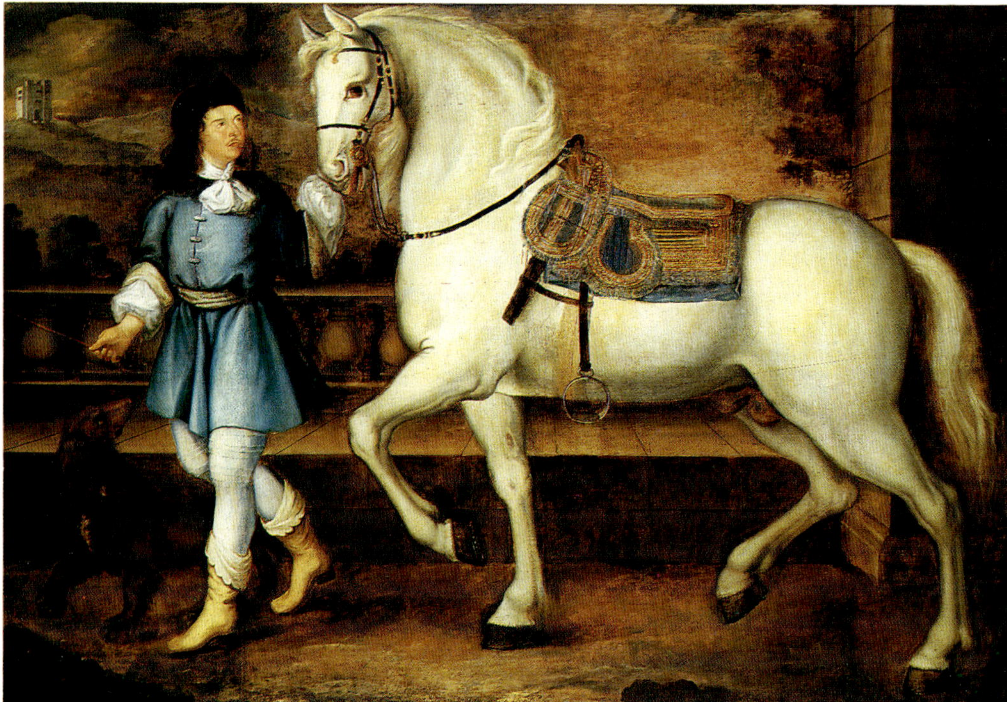

Unknown artist, *Grey Stallion and Attendant*, 1666. This magnificent painting of a stallion is a powerful symbol of the owner's wealth and status.

headlong charge of British cavalry at the Battle of Waterloo (1815) was captured in all its violence and colour by Lady Butler, one of the few women artists to show the horse in action (*see* Plate 23). On the land and in the cities, however, large breeds were still valued for their pulling power. Harnessed between the shafts of the plough, the horse proved a more intelligent and adaptable draught animal than the ox, and its role in the agricultural revolution was reflected in paintings of country life. A particular sympathy for horses of all kinds characterized the art of the French painter Géricault, who made a number of studies of ordinary working animals, as well as creating imaginary scenes of frenzied emotion more Romantic in feel.

By the middle of the nineteenth century, increased wealth brought the delights of horse-drawn travel within the reach of many more people. As Henri (Le Douanier) Rousseau showed in his delightful naive style, whole families could go on an outing in a pony-cart (*see* Plate 22). On the sporting field trotting became a popular minority sport, particularly in the United States, although conventional racing never lost its attraction for both participants and spectators. Few artists have captured the movement and excitement of the racecourse with as much immediacy as the French

Impressionist painter Degas (*see* Plate 21). Although his appreciation of the horses' vigour and line is evident, he never pictured them as solitary figures, in the way that Stubbs and Géricault had done, but made them part of an overall scene.

Now that machines have replaced the horse in so many areas of life, it has come to assume a primarily symbolic role in the artist's imagination. The vivid yellow animals of Franz Marc enjoy the carefree existence of wild creatures, unfettered by human contact (*see* Plate 24). Their magical innocence is a reminder that, however much humans may have loved and exploited them, horses retain their own grace and spirit.

THE PLATES

PLATE 1

Simone Martini (*c.* 1285–1344)

Guido Riccio da Fogliano

How the horse dominated the mind of the early races, especially of the Mediterranean! You were a lord if you had a horse. Far back, far back in our dark soul the horse prances... The horse, the horse! The symbol of surging potency and power of movement, of action, in man.

From *Apocalypse*
D H LAWRENCE (1885–1930)

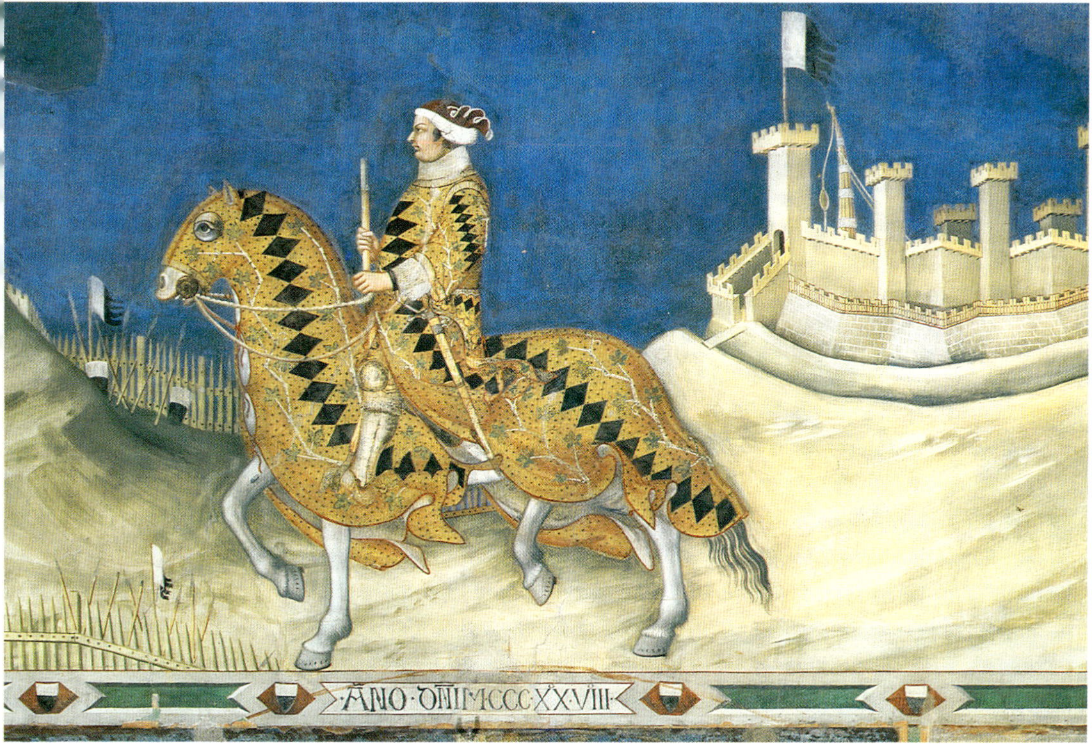
ĀNO·DÑI·MCCCXXVIII

PLATE 2

Paolo Uccello (*c.* 1397–1475)

The Battle of San Romano

The fiery courser, when he hears from far
The sprightly trumpets, and the shouts of war,
Pricks up his ears; and, trembling with delight,
Shifts place, and paws, and hopes the promised fight.
On his right shoulder his thick mane reclined,
Ruffles at speed, and dances in the wind.
His horny hoofs are jetted black and round;
His chine is double; starting with a bound
He turns the turf, and shakes the solid ground.

From *The Georgics*
VIRGIL (70–19 BC)
Trans. John Dryden (1631–1700)

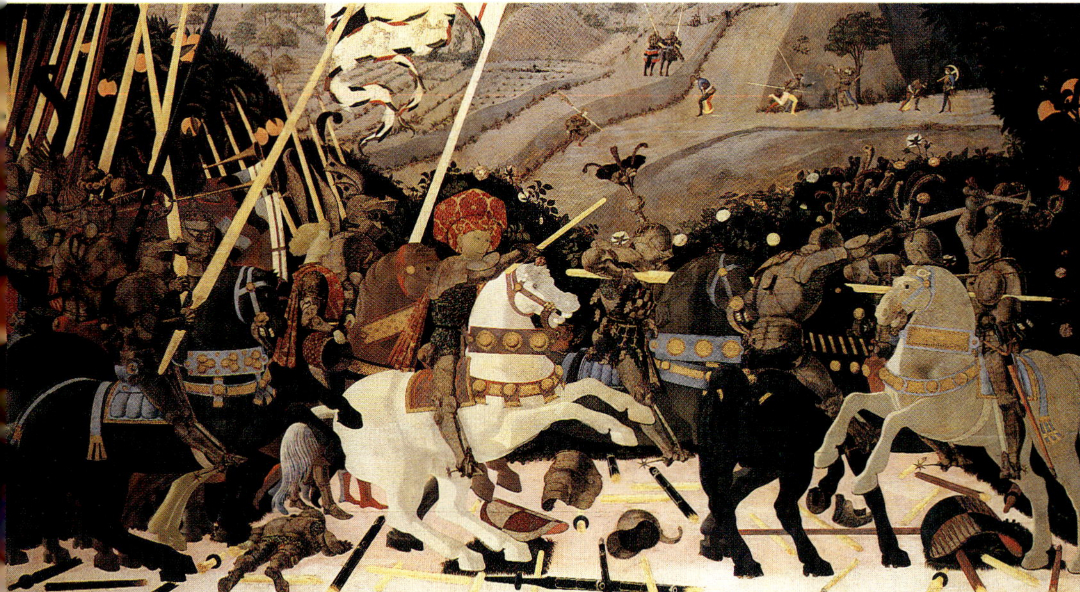

PLATE 3

Andrea Mantegna (*c.* 1431–1506)

The Duke's Grooms

DETAIL

The colt, that for a stallion is designed,
By sure presages shows his generous kind:
Of able body, sound of limb and wind,
Upright he walks, on pasterns firm and straight;
His motions easy; prancing in his gait;
The first to lead the way, to tempt the flood,
To pass the bridge unknown, nor fear the trembling wood;
Dauntless at empty noises; lofty necked;
Sharp-headed, barrel-bellied, broadly backed:
Brawny his chest, and deep, his colour gray;
For beauty, dappled, or the brightest bay.

From *The Georgics*
VIRGIL (70–19 BC)
Trans. John Dryden (1631–1700)

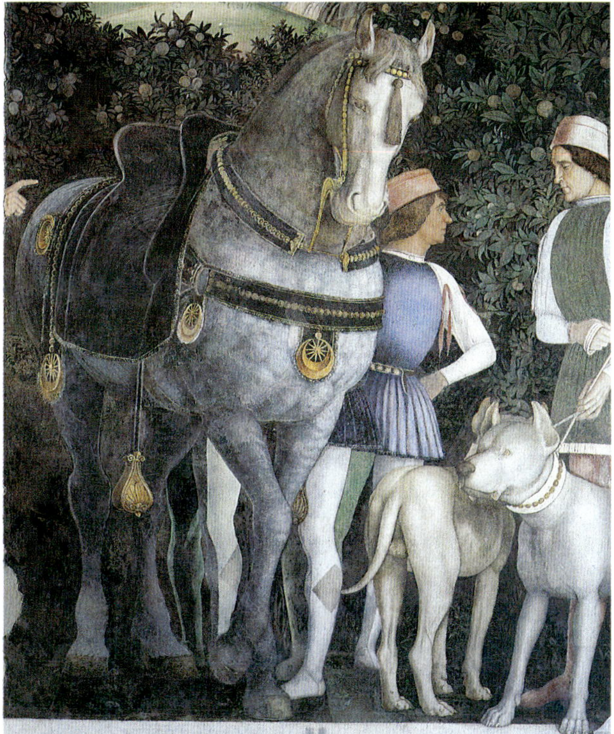

PLATE 4

Studio of François Clouet (*c.* 1522–72)

Francis I of France on Horseback

Comely and calm he rides
Hard by his own Whitehall:
Only the night wind glides:
No crowds, nor rebels, brawl.
Gone, too, his Court: and yet
The stars his courtiers are:
Stars in their stations set;
And every wandering star.
Alone he rides, alone,
The fair and fatal king;
Dark night is all his own,
That strange and solemn thing.

From *By the Statue of King Charles at Charing Cross*
LIONEL JOHNSON (1867–1902)

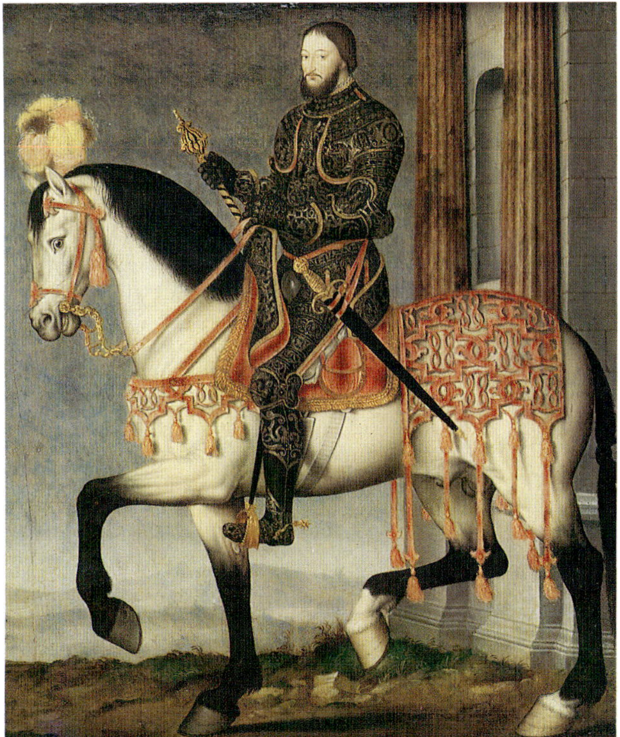

PLATE 5

Nicolas Poussin (1594–1665)

Meleager and Atalanta Hunting

DETAIL

Imperiously he leaps, he neighs, he bounds,
And now his woven girths he breaks asunder;
The bearing earth with his hard hoof he wounds;
Whose hollow womb resounds like heaven's thunder;
The iron bit he crusheth 'tween his teeth,
Controlling what he was controllèd with.

His ears up-prick'd; his braided hanging mane
Upon his compass'd crest now stand on end.
His nostrils drink the air, and forth again,
As from a furnace, vapours doth he send:
His eye, which scornfully glisters like fire,
Shows his hot courage and his high desire.

From *Venus and Adonis*
WILLIAM SHAKESPEARE (1564–1616)

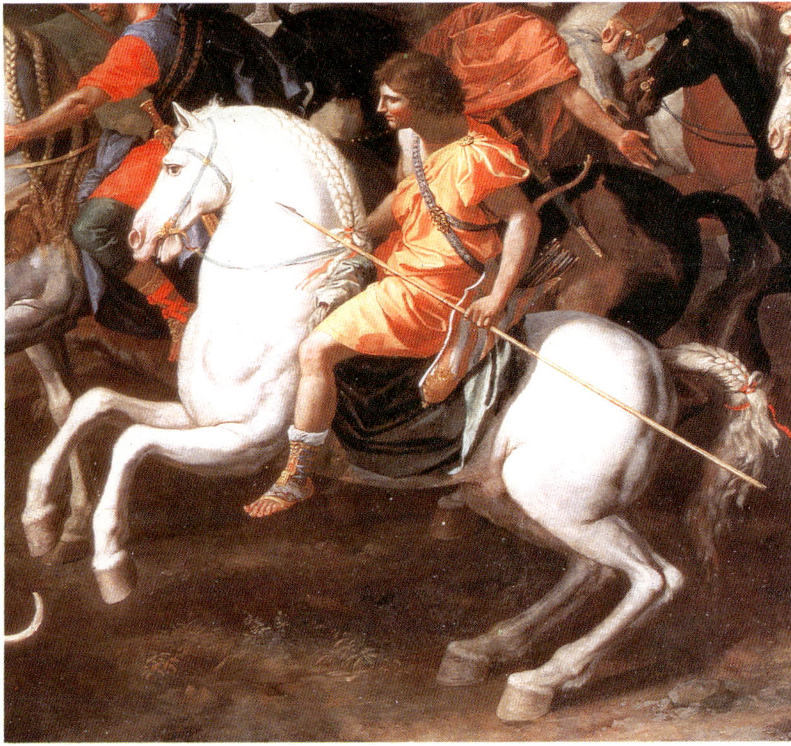

PLATE 6

English School (17th century)

A Prancing Stallion

The wanton Courser this, with Reins unbound,
Breaks from his Stall, and beats the trembling Ground;
Pamper'd and proud, he seeks the wonted Tides,
And laves, in Height of Blood, his shining Sides;
His Head now freed, he tosses to the Skies;
His Mane dishevel'd o'er his Shoulders flies;
He snuffs the Females in the distant Plain,
And springs, exulting, to his Fields again.

From *The Iliad*
HOMER (8th century BC)
Trans. Alexander Pope (1688–1744)

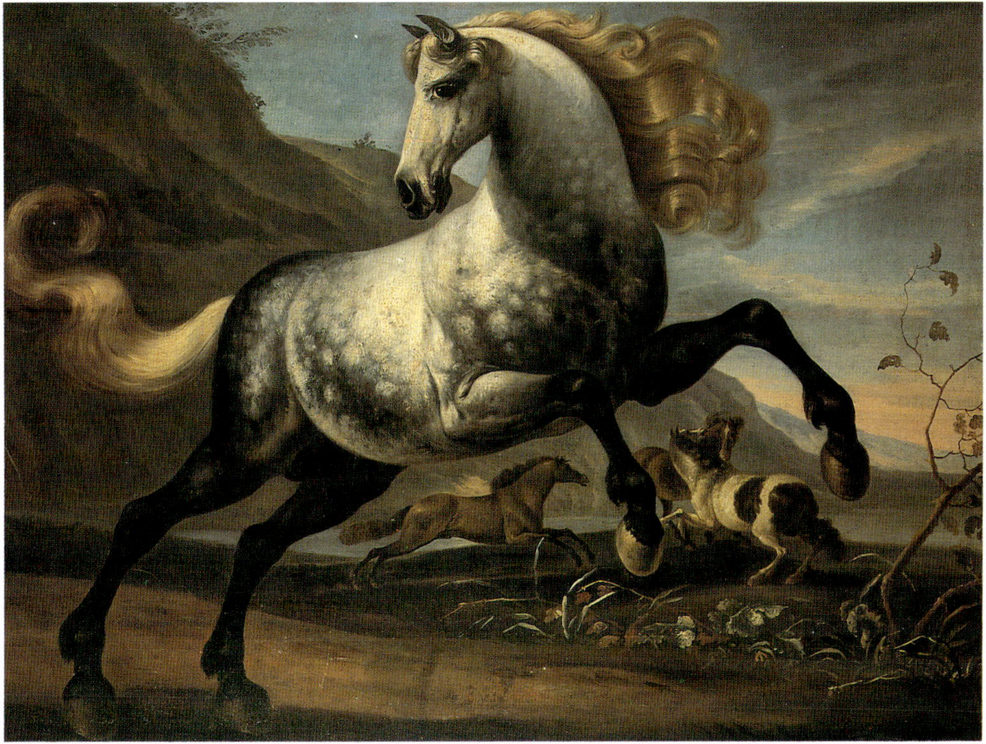

PLATE 7

Firdausi's Shahnama (17th century) Persian Manuscript

A Battle Scene

DETAIL

Let me tell you further that this province produces a sturdy breed of horses, which are exported when young for sale in India… The horsemen here ride with long stirrups after the French fashion – long, that is, in contrast to the short stirrups favoured by the Tartars and most other races who go in for archery, since they use their stirrups for standing upright when they shoot.

From *The Travels of Marco Polo*
MARCO POLO (1254–1324)

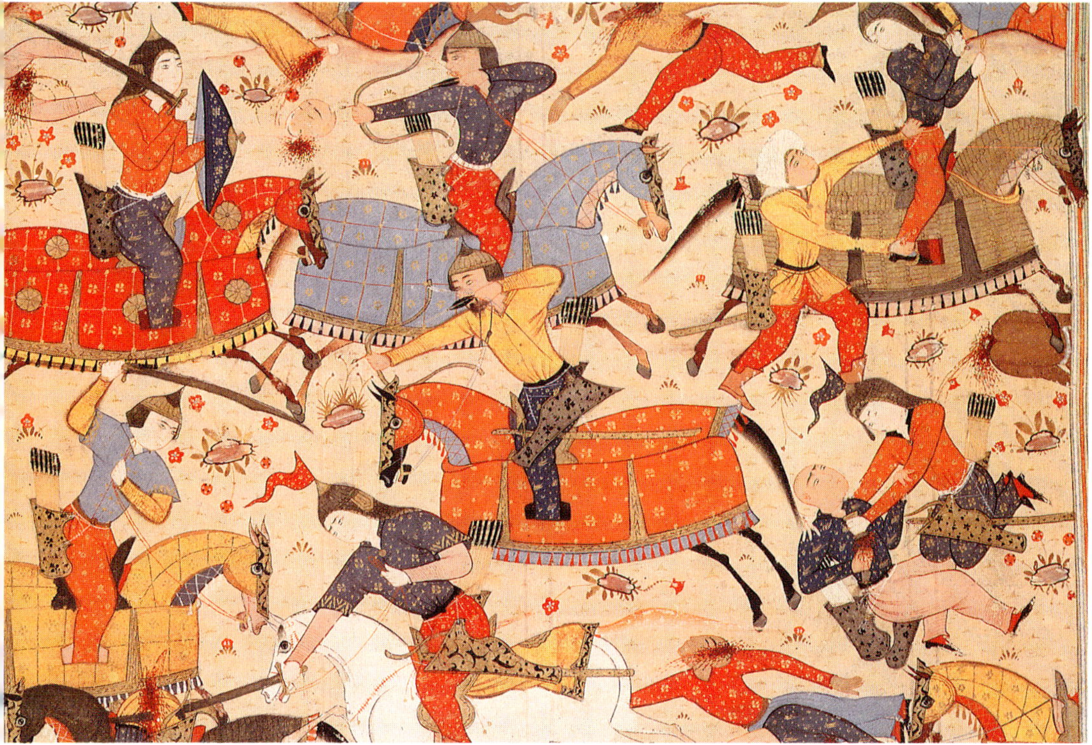

PLATE 9

George Stubbs (1724–1806)

Mares and Foals without a Background

My horses understand me tolerably well; I converse with them at least four hours every day. They are strangers to bridle or saddle; they live in great amity with me, and friendship to each other.

From *Gulliver's Travels*
JONATHAN SWIFT (1667–1745)

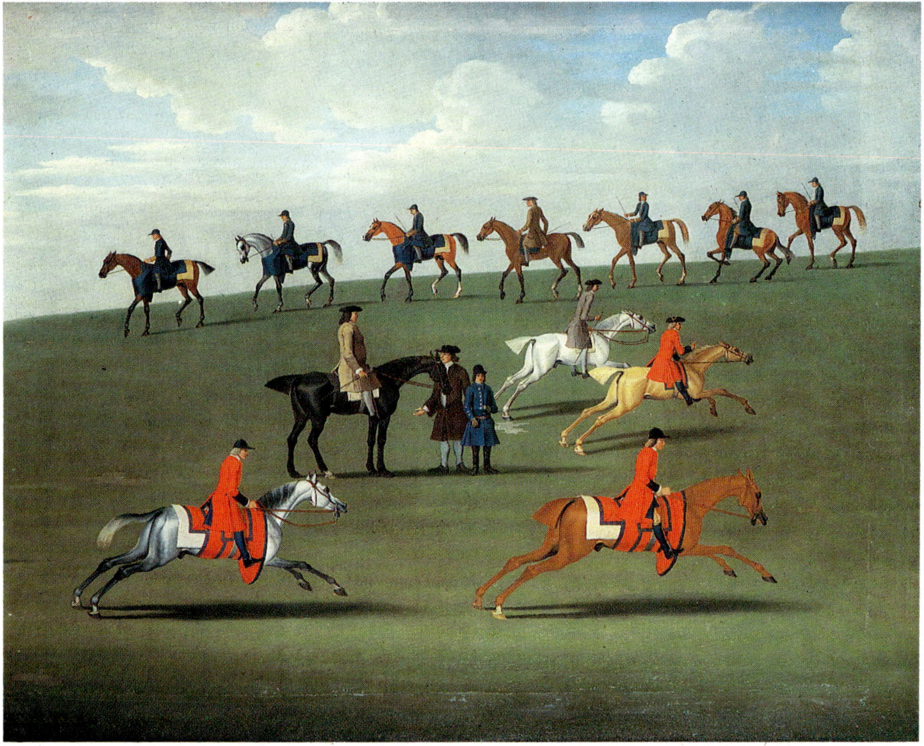

PLATE 8

James Seymour (1702–52)

Racehorses Exercising in a Landscape

Today, all day, I rode upon the down,
With hounds and horsemen, a brave company.
On this side in its glory lay the sea,
On that the Sussex weald, a sea of brown.
The wind was light, and brightly the sun shone,
And still we galloped on from gorse to gorse.
And once, when checked, a thrush sang, and my horse
Pricked his quick ears as to a sound unknown.

From *St Valentine's Day*
WILFRED SCAWEN BLUNT (1840–1922)

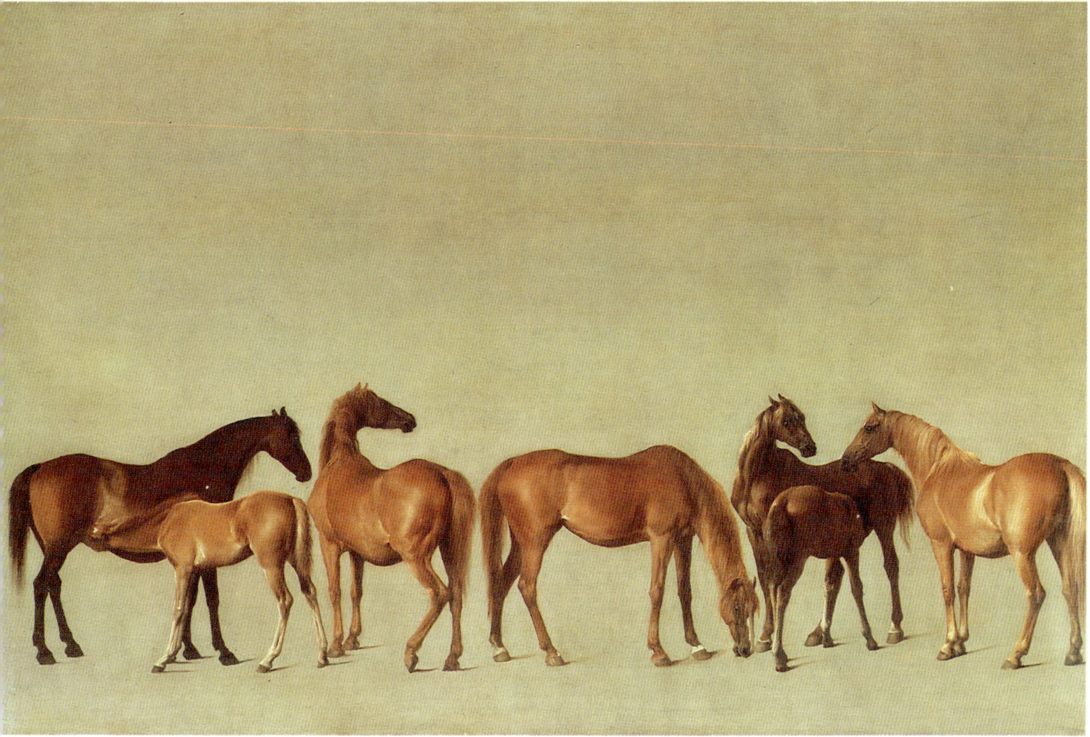

PLATE 10

George Stubbs (1724–1806)

Soldiers of the 10th Light Dragoons

And there was mounting in hot haste: the steed,
The mustering squadron, and the clattering car,
Went pouring forward with impetuous speed
And swiftly forming in the ranks of war;
And the deep thunder peal on peal afar;
And near, the beat of the alarming drum
Roused up the soldier ere the morning star;
While throng'd the citizens with terror dumb,
Or whispering, with white lips – 'The foe! they come!
they come!'

From *Childe Harold*
LORD BYRON (1788–1824)

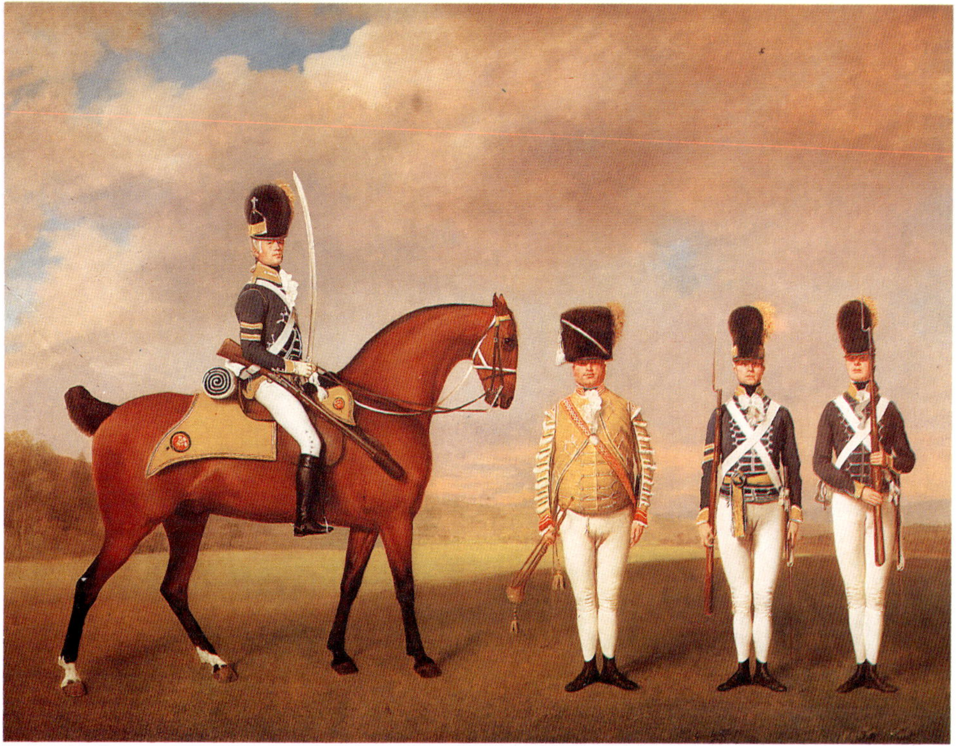

PLATE 11

George Stubbs (1724–1806)

Horse Frightened by a Lion

DETAIL

Round-hoof'd, short-jointed, fetlocks shag and long,
Broad breast, full eye, small head, and nostril wide,
High crest, short ears, straight legs, and passing strong,
Thin mane, thick tail, broad buttocks, tender hide:
Look, what a horse should have he did not lack,
Save a proud rider on so proud a back.

From *Venus and Adonis*
WILLIAM SHAKESPEARE (1564–1616)

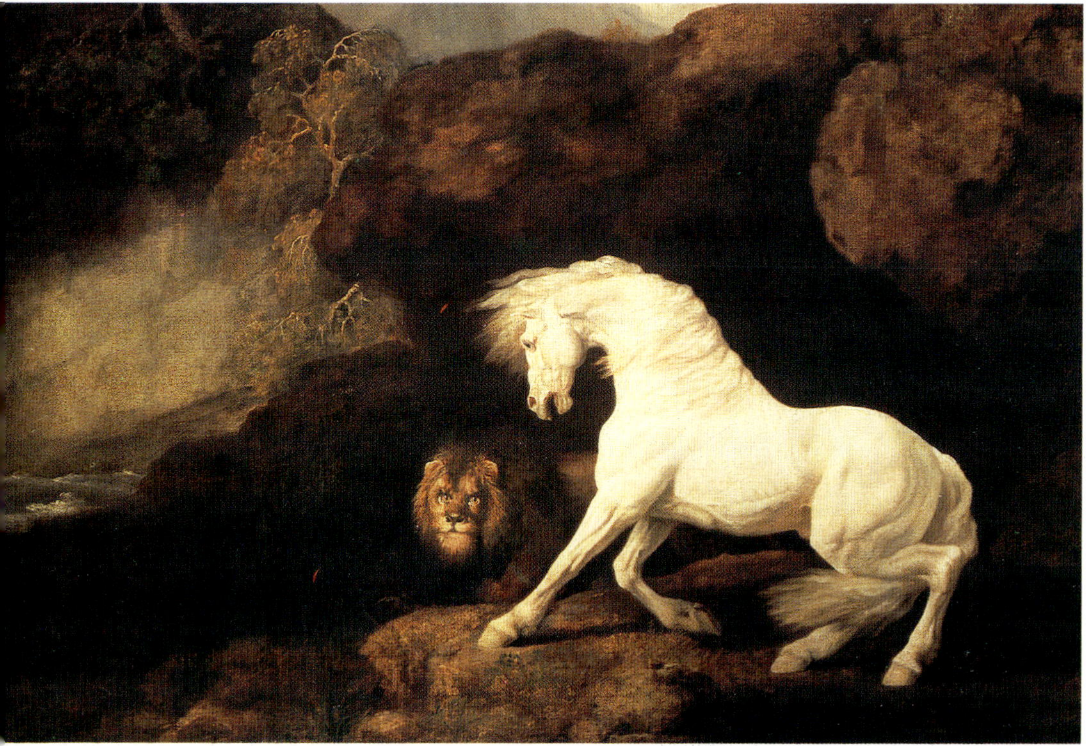

PLATE 12

William Blake (1757–1827)

Pity

Gallop apace, you fiery-footed steeds,
Towards Phoebus' lodging: such a wagoner
As Phaeton would whip you to the west,
And bring in cloudy night immediately.

From *Romeo and Juliet*
WILLIAM SHAKESPEARE (1564–1616)

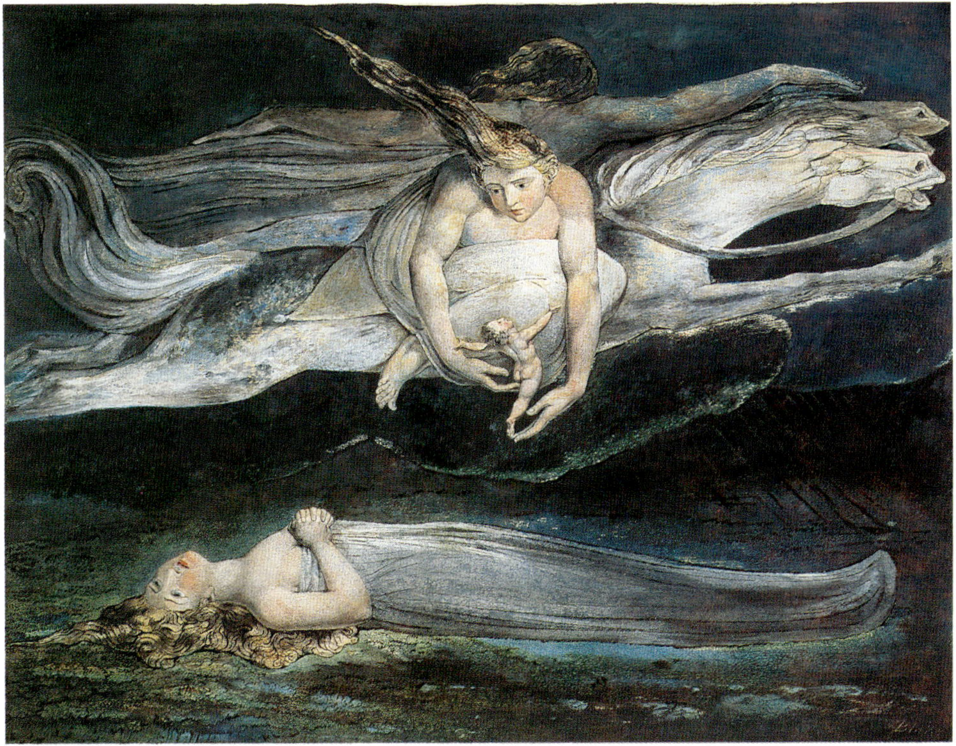

PLATE 13

Henry Alken (*c.* 1785–1851)

Racing Scene

The first favourite was never heard of, the second favourite was never seen after the distance post, all the ten-to-oners were in the rear, and a dark horse, which had never been thought of… rushed past the grand stand to sweeping triumph.

From *The Young Duke*
BENJAMIN DISRAELI (1804–81)

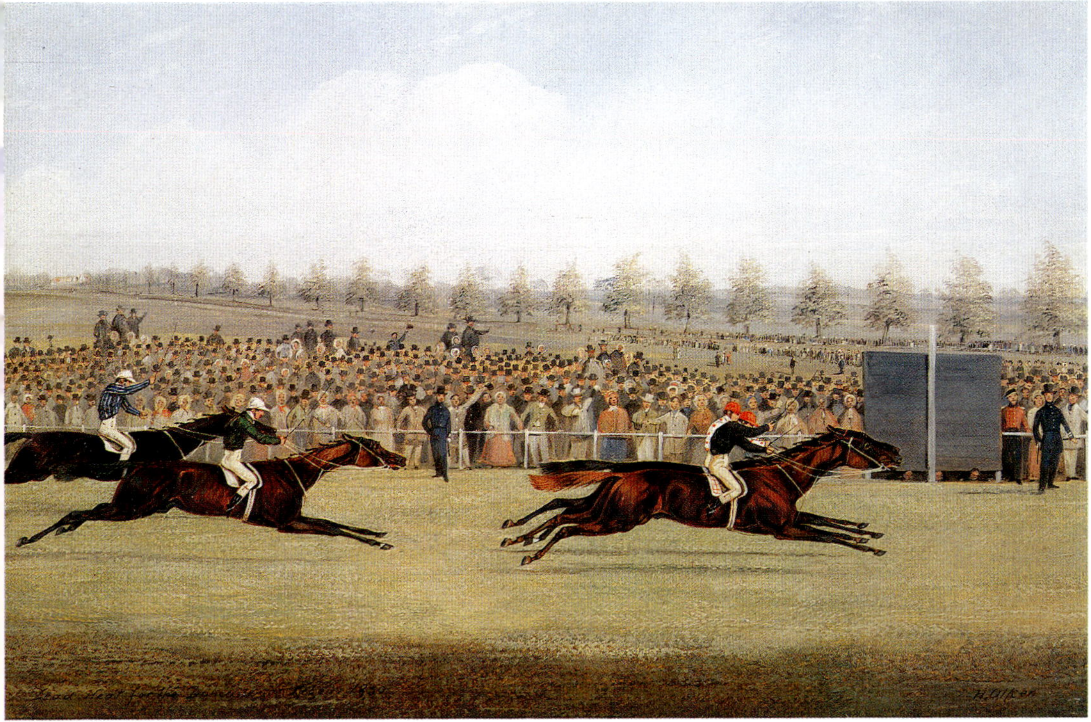
H. Alken

PLATE 14

Théodore Géricault (1791–1824)

English Butcher mounted on a Horse

O barbarous men! your cruel breasts assuage;
Why vent ye on the generous steed your rage?
Does not his service earn your daily bread?
Your wives, your children, by his labours fed!

From *Trivia*
JOHN GAY (1685–1732)

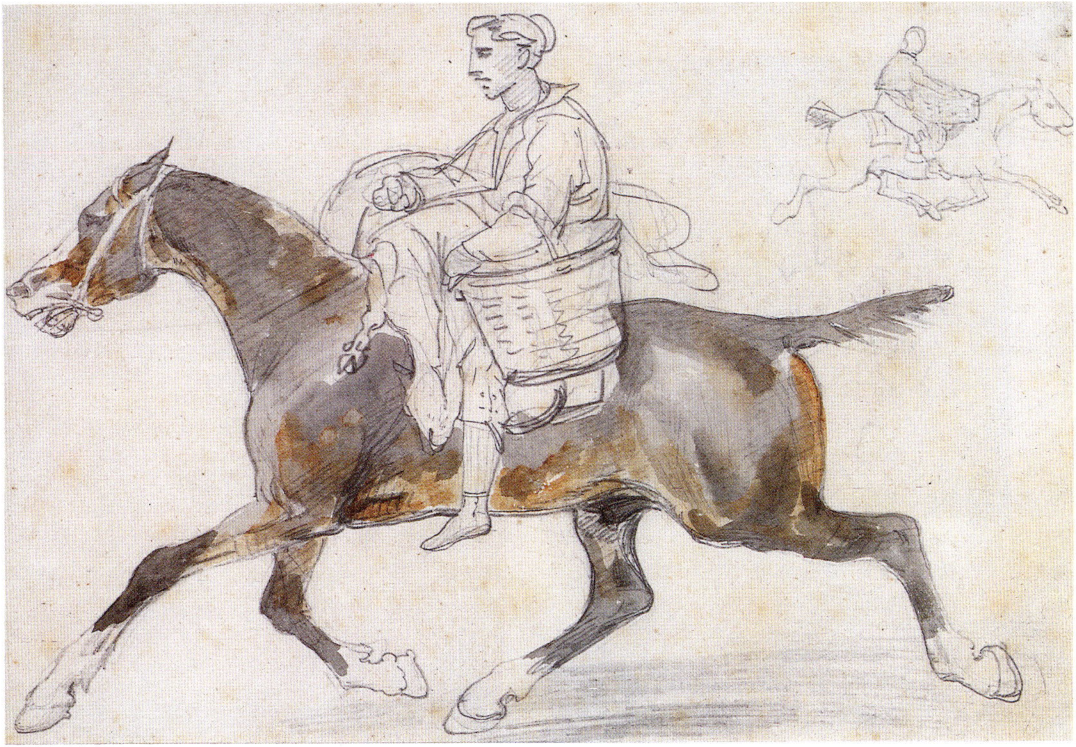

PLATE 15

Kalighat School, Calcutta (*c.* 1830)

Jockeys Racing

The valiant horse races best, at the barrier's fall,
when he has others to follow and overtake.

From *Ars Amatoria*
OVID (43 BC – AD 17)

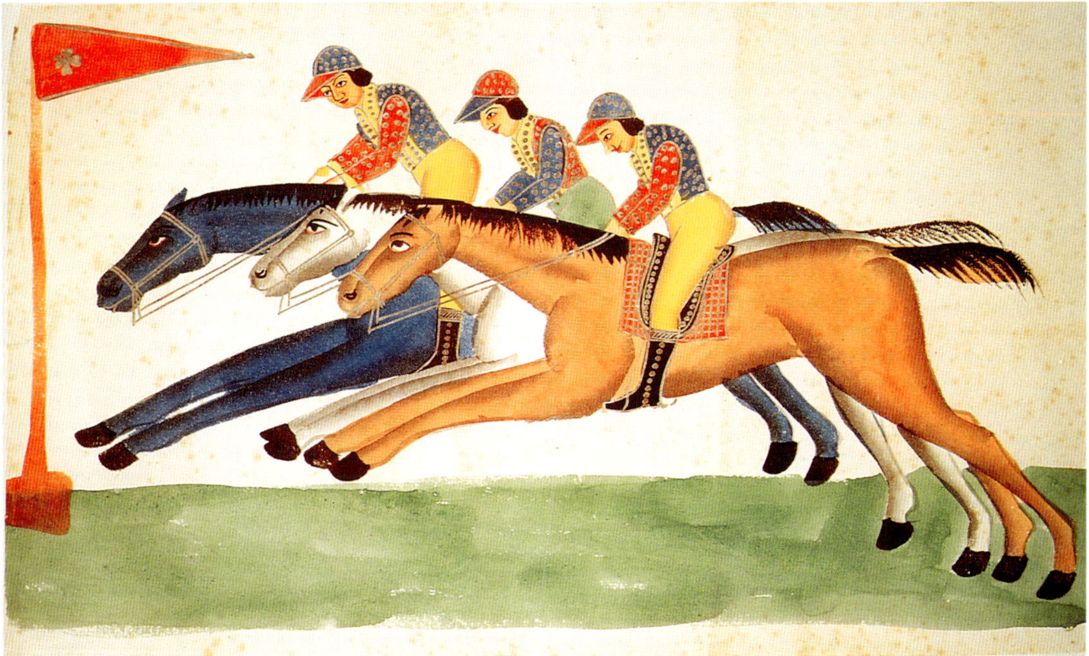

PLATE 16

John Herring Snr. (1795–1865)

Touchstones, a Bay Racehorse in a Loosebox

They say Princes learn no art truly, but the art of horsemanship.
The reason is, the brave beast is no flatterer. He will
throw a Prince as soon as his groom.

From *Explorata: Illiteratus Princeps*
BEN JONSON (1573–1637)

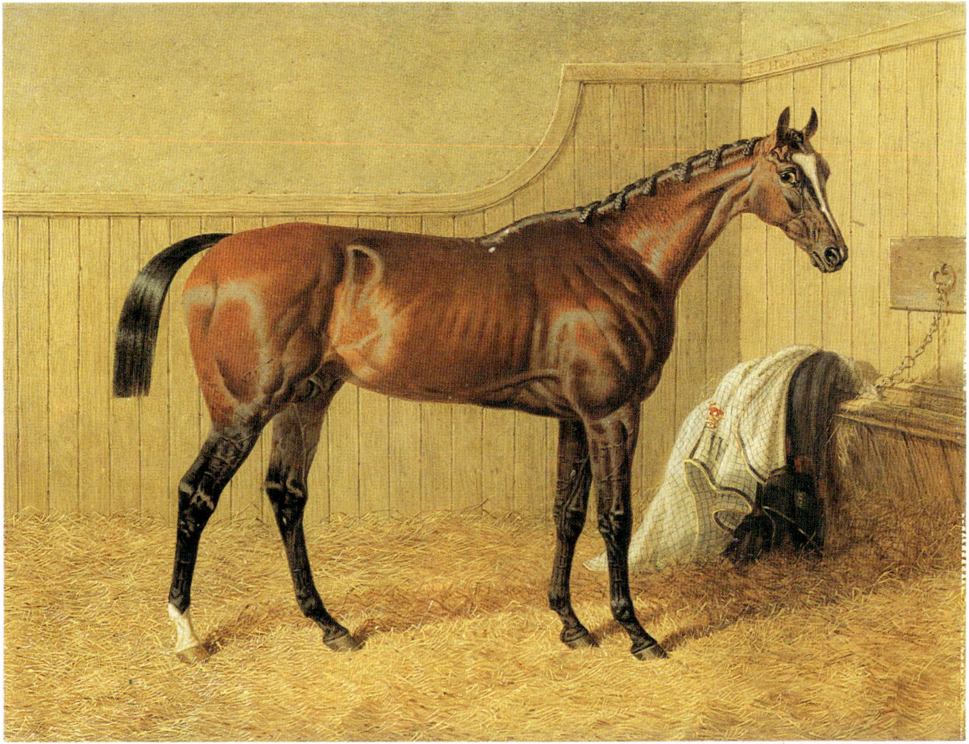

PLATE 17

John Leech (1817–64)

'Come hup! I say–You ugly brute!'

The Brogue had been variously described in sale catalogues as a light-weight hunter, a lady's hack, and, more simply, but still with a touch of imagination, as a useful brown gelding, standing 15.1. Toby Mullet had ridden him for four seasons with the West Wessex; you can ride almost any sort of horse with the West Wessex as long as it is an animal that knows the country. The Brogue knew the country intimately, having personally created most of the gaps there were to be met with in banks and hedges for many miles round.

From *The Brogue*
SAKI (H H MUNRO) (1870–1916)

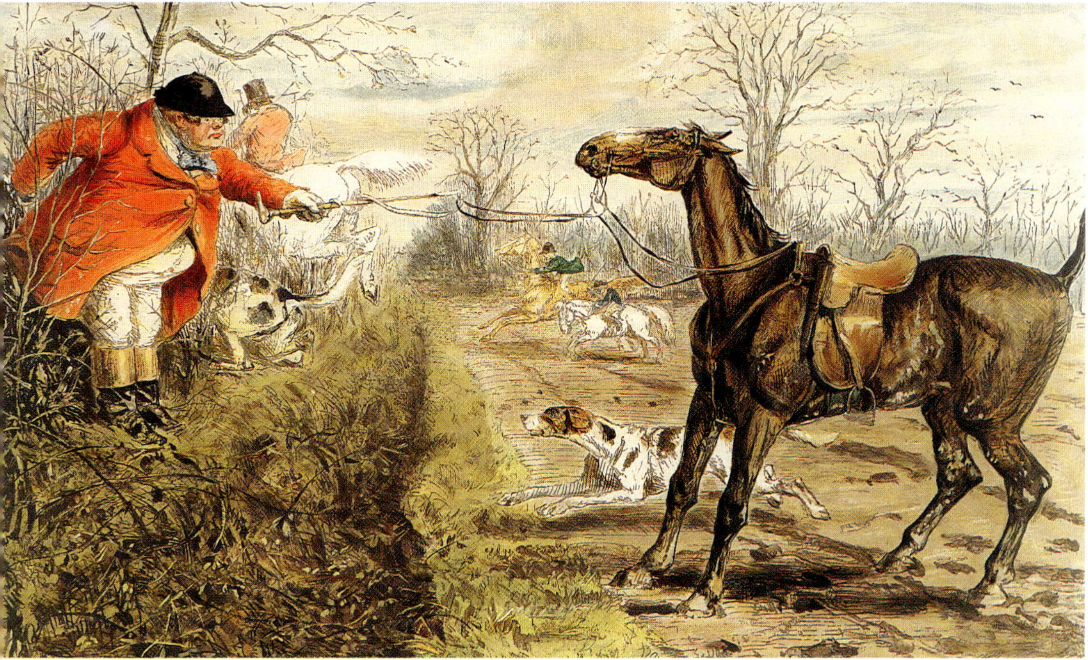

PLATE 18

George Horlor (*fl.* 1849–91)

Portrait of Favourites

Men are generally more careful of the breed of their horses and dogs than of their children.

From *Some Fruits of Solitude*
WILLIAM PENN (1644–1718)

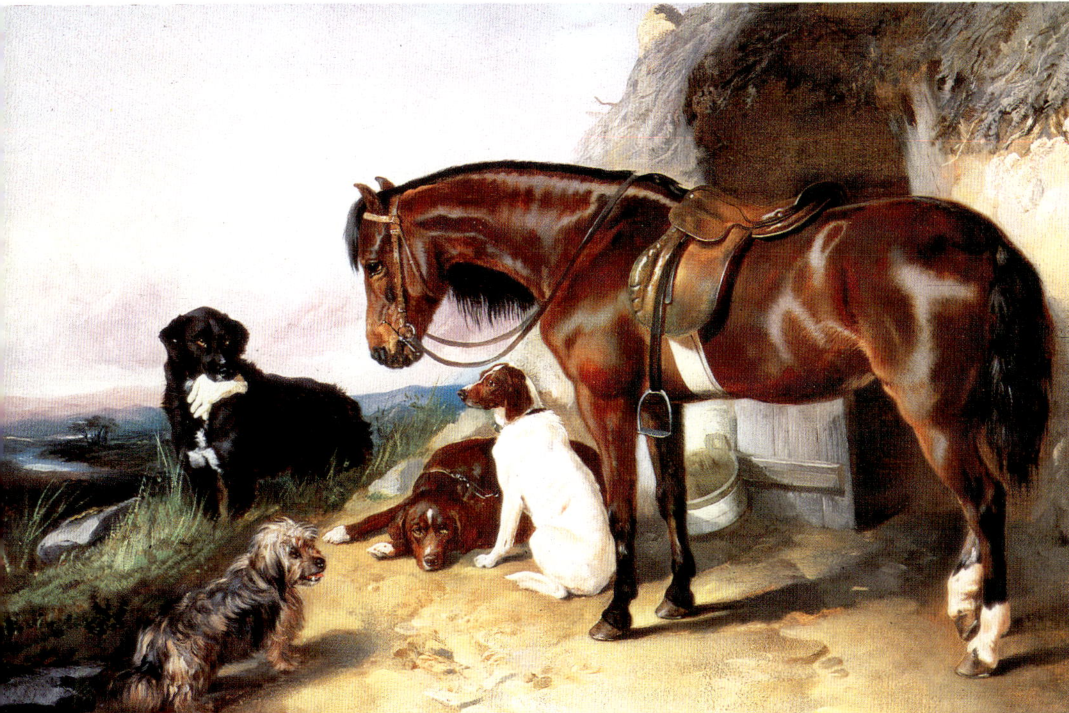

PLATE 19

Currier and Ives (1866)

The Celebrated Trotting Stallion, George Wilkes

The first was a white horse, as white as the milk,
The next was a grey horse, as soft as the silk,
The next was a black horse, as sleek as a mole,
The next was a brown horse, like diamonds did show.
As I go a'driving all on the highway,
When light goes my load, then I feed them with hay,
And give them some water when we comes to a pond
And after they've drunk, boys, go steady along.

From *The Carter*
ANON

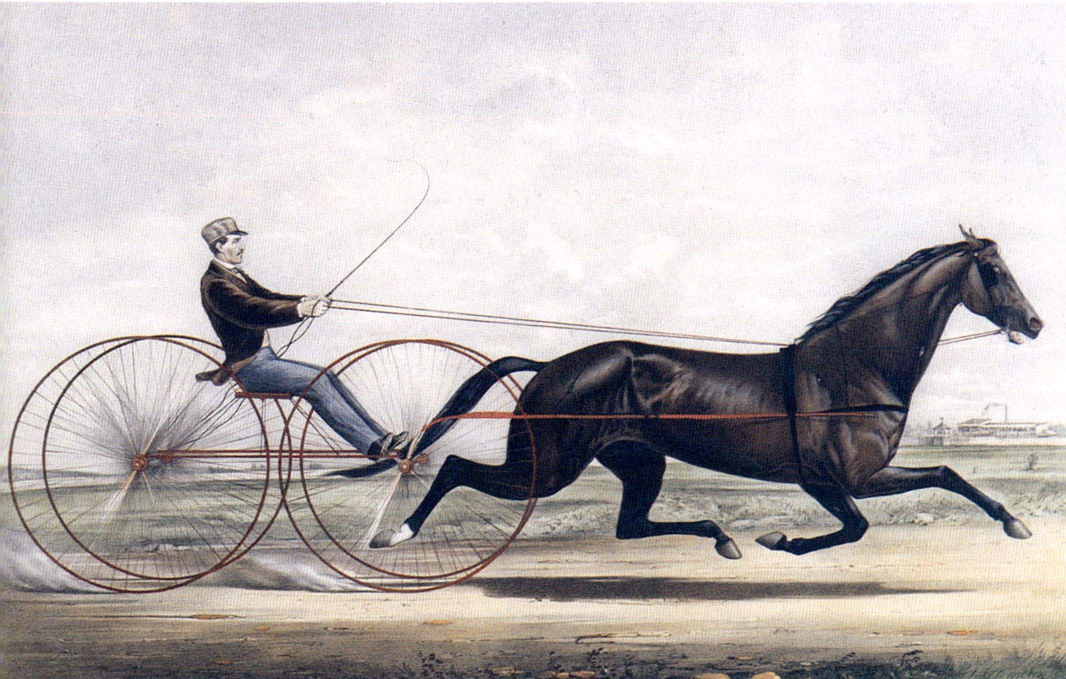

PLATE 20

Charles Emile Jacque (1813–94)

Ploughing

Over the broad hill creeps a beam,
Like hope that gilds a good man's brow;
And now ascends the nostril-stream
Of stalwart horses come to plough.
Ye rigid Ploughmen, bear in mind
Your labour is for future hours:
Advance – spare not – nor look behind –
Plough deep and straight with all your powers.

From *The Plough*
R H HORNE (1803–84)

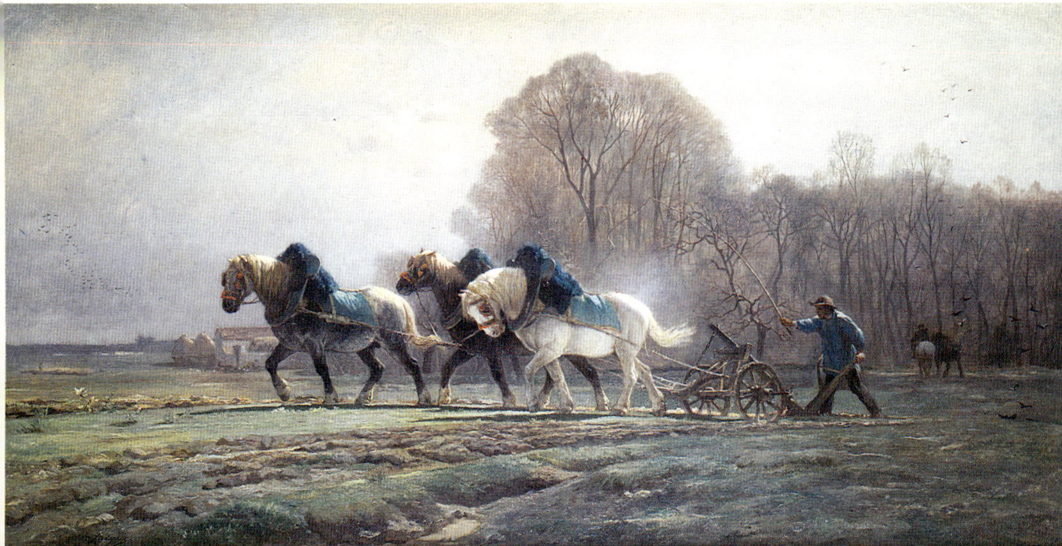

PLATE 21

Edgar Degas (1834–1917)

Jockeys in Front of the Grandstands

There where the course is,
Delight makes all of the one mind,
The riders upon the galloping horses,
The crowd that closes in behind:
We too had good attendance once,
Hearers and hearteners of the work;
Aye, horsemen for companions,
Before the merchant and the clerk
Breathed on the world with timid breath.

From *At Galway Races*
W B YEATS (1865–1939)

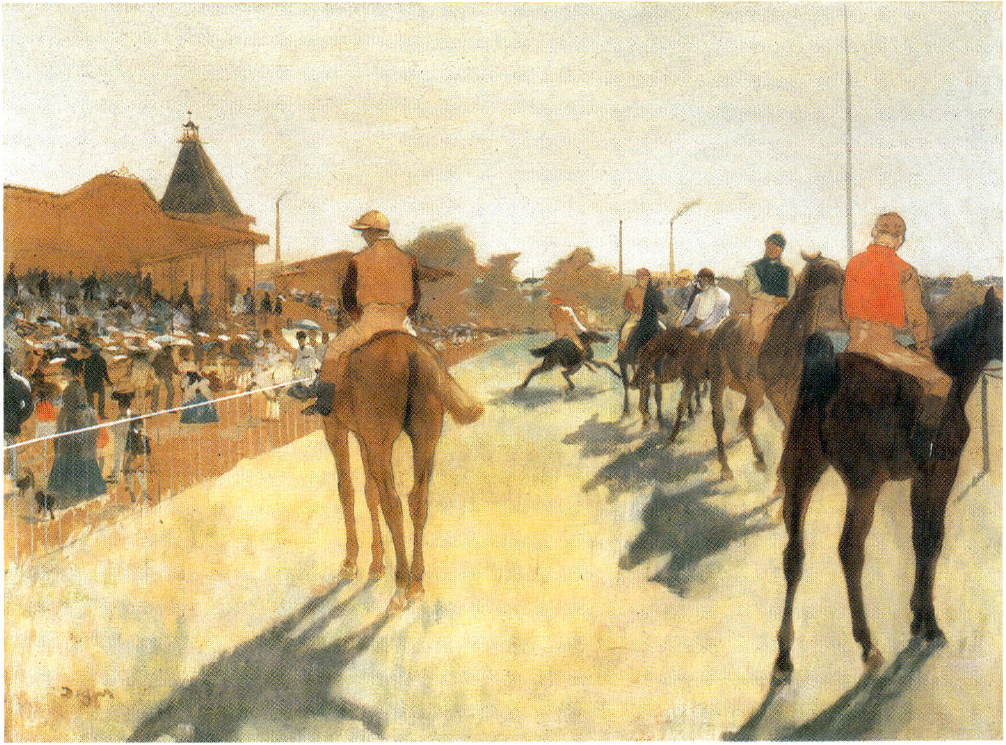

PLATE 22

Henri Rousseau (1844–1910)

Father Juniet's Cart

Of all the pleasant ways
To pass an afternoon,
Is in a pony chaise
One sultry day in June.
To drive between the trees
In Hyde Park round and round,
It brings a pleasant sense of ease
In spinning o'er the ground.
The men raise hats to me,
I mean, the men I know,
They smile, kiss hands, then laugh to see
The flying pony go.

From *Driving in the Park*
ANON

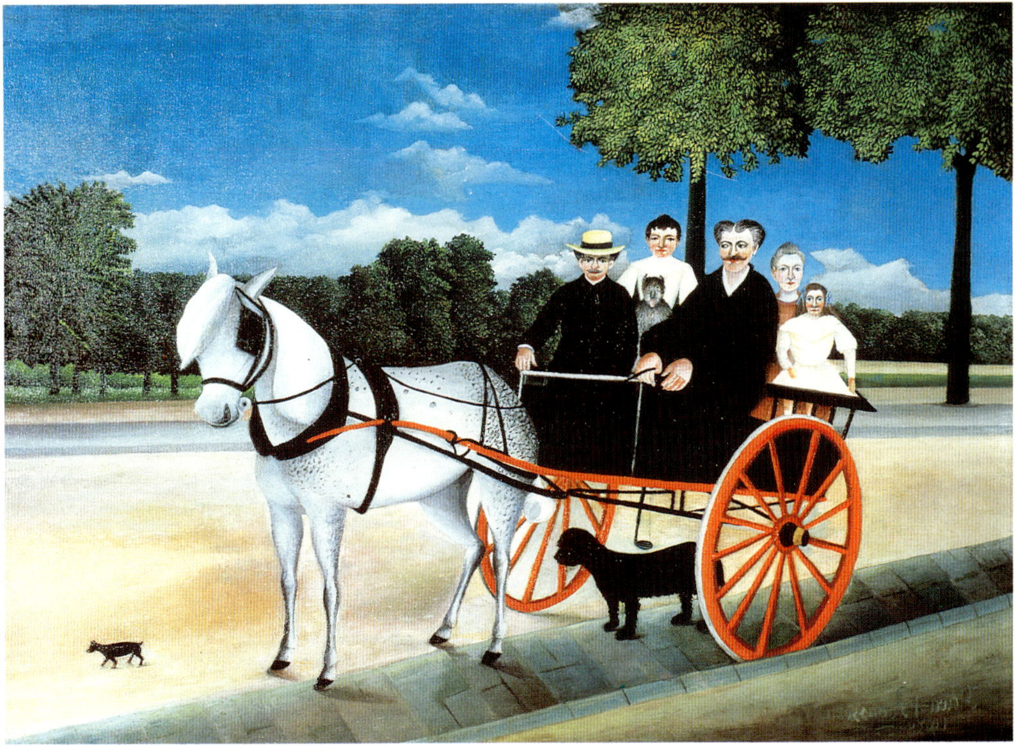

PLATE 23

Elizabeth, Lady Butler (1846–1933)

Scotland for Ever

DETAIL

Cannon to right of them,
Cannon to left of them,
Cannon in front of them
Volley'd and thunder'd;
Storm'd at with shot and shell,
While horse and hero fell,
They that had fought so well
Came thro' the jaws of Death
Back from the mouth of Hell...

From *The Charge of the Light Brigade*
ALFRED, LORD TENNYSON (1809–92)

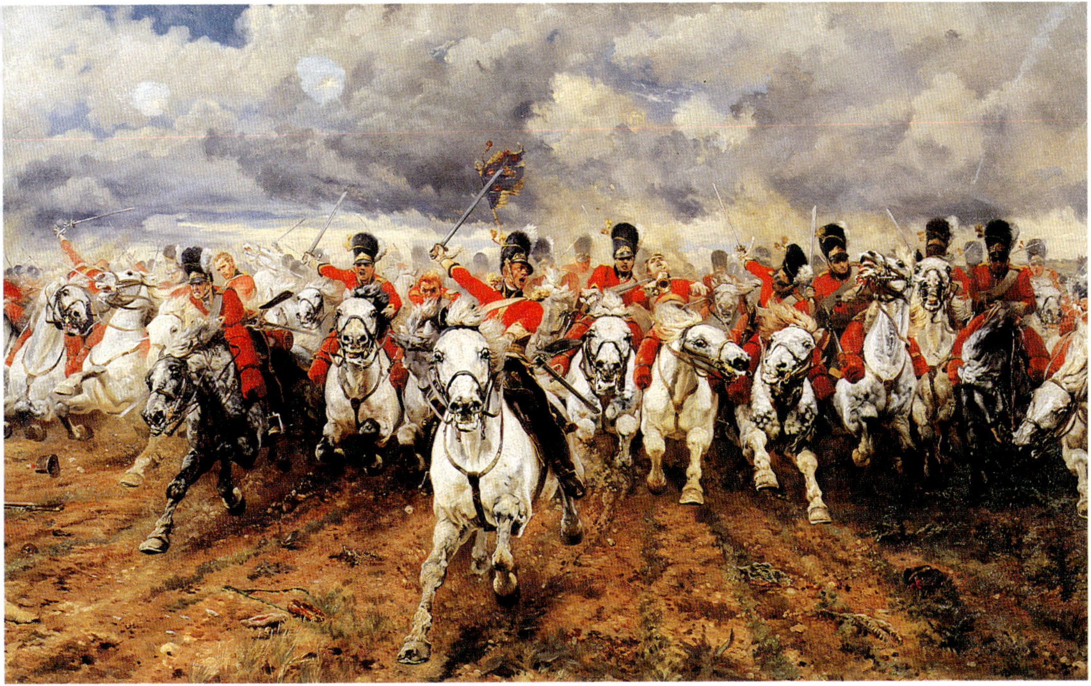

PLATE 24

Franz Marc (1880–1916)

Little Yellow Horses

It is a beast for Perseus: he is pure air and fire; and the dull elements of earth and water never appear in him, but only in patient stillness while his rider mounts him: he is, indeed, a horse; and other jades you may call beasts... It is the prince of palfreys; his neigh is like the bidding of a monarch, and his countenance enforces homage.

From *King Henry the Fifth*
WILLIAM SHAKESPEARE (1564–1616)

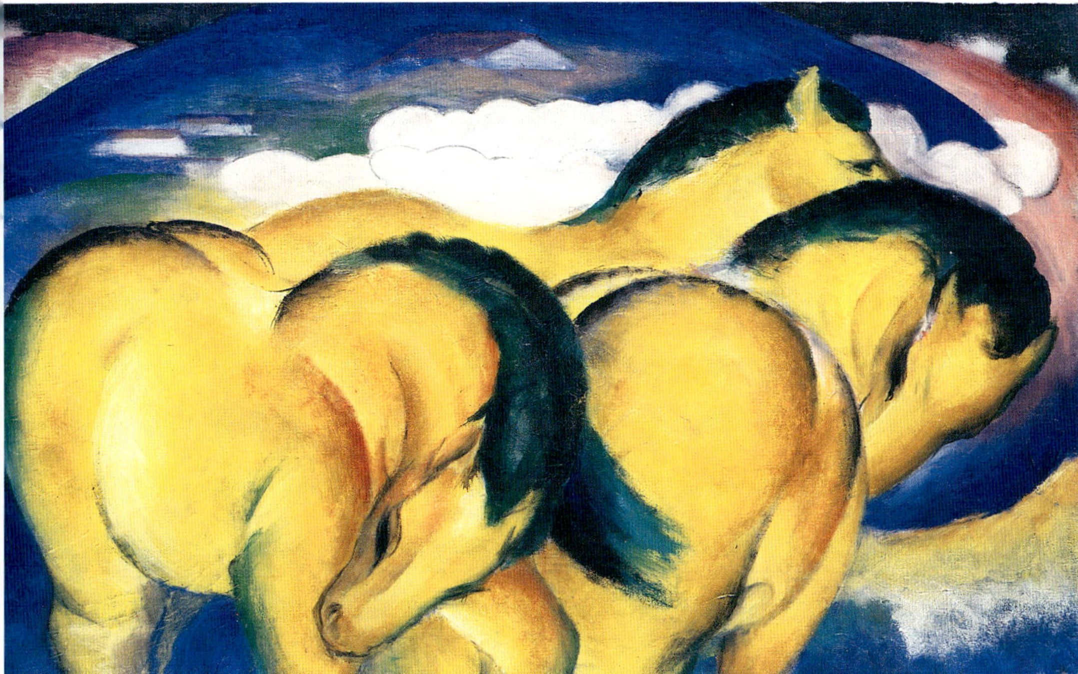

PLATE 25

Alfred Munnings (1878–1959)

The Poppy Field

'O saddle to me my milk-white steed,
And go and fetch my pony, O!
That I may ride and seek my bride
Who is gone with the wraggle taggle gipsies, O!'
O he rode high and he rode low,
He rode through wood and copses too,
Until he came to an open field,
And there he espied his lady, O!

From *The Wraggle Taggle Gipsies*
ANON

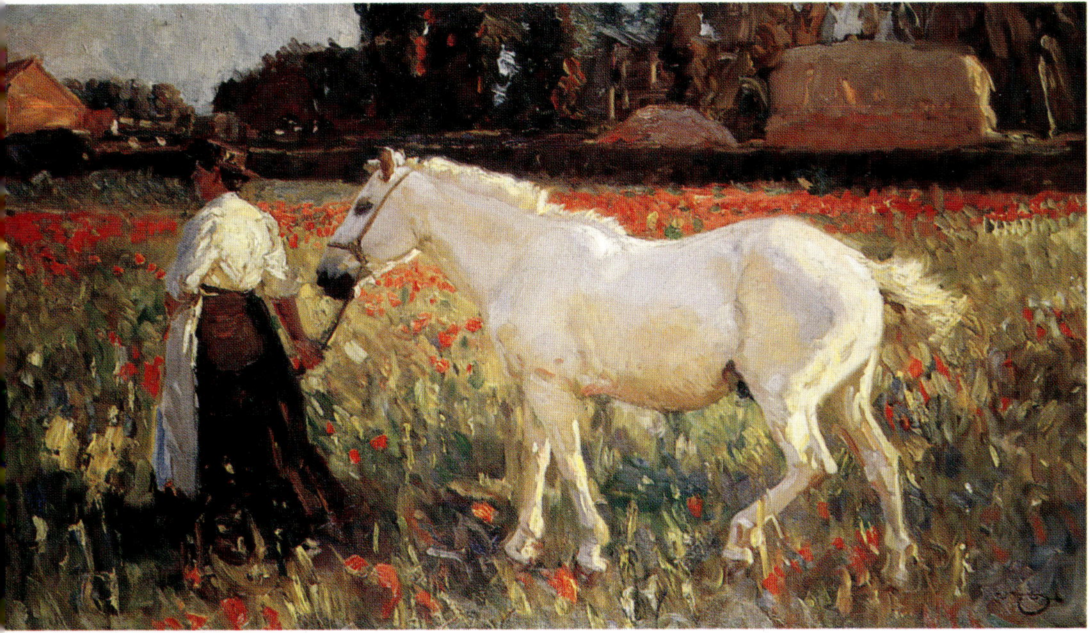

PICTURE ACKNOWLEDGEMENTS

The author and publishers would like to thank the following artists, collectors, galleries and photographic libraries for permission to reproduce their illustrations:—

INTRODUCTION
Frontispiece: Christie's, London (Bridgeman Art Library, London)
Museo Nationale, Naples (Scala, Florence)
Palazzo del Té, Mantua (Scala)
Lyme Park, Cheshire (National Trust Photographic Library)

PLATES
1 Palazzo Publico, Siena (Scala)
2 The National Gallery, London
3 Palazzo Ducale, Mantua (E. T. Archive, London)
4 Bearstead Collection, Upton House, Warwickshire (National Trust Photographic Library)
5 Prado, Madrid (Bridgeman Art Library)
6 Christie's, London (Bridgeman Art Library)
7 Christie's, London (Bridgeman Art Library)
8 Christie's, London (Bridgeman Art Library)
9 Private Collection (Bridgeman Art Library)
10 The Royal Collection © 1994 Her Majesty Queen Elizabeth II
11 Board of Trustees of the National Museums & Galleries on Merseyside: Walker Art Gallery, Liverpool
12 The Tate Gallery, London
13 Oscar & Peter Johnson Ltd, London (Bridgeman Art Library)
14 Christie's, London (Bridgeman Art Library)
15 Courtesy of the Board of Trustees of the Victoria & Albert Museum, London (E. T. Archive)
16 Christie's, London (Bridgeman Art Library)
17 Courtesy of the Board of Trustees of the Victoria & Albert Museum, London
18 Cheltenham Art Gallery & Museums, Gloucestershire (Bridgeman Art Library)
19 Hall of Fame of the Trotter (Bridgeman Art Library)
20 Christie's, London (Bridgeman Art Library)
21 Musée d'Orsay, Paris (Bridgeman Art Library)
22 Jeu de Paume, Paris (Bridgeman Art Library)
23 Leeds City Art Galleries
24 Staatsgalerie, Stuttgart (Artothek, Munich)
25 & Cover (detail) Dundee Art Gallery © Sir Alfred Munnings Art Museum, Dedham (Bridgeman Art Library)